LITTLE BOOK OF GIN

An exclusive edition for

ALLSORTED.

This edition first published in Great Britain in 2024
by Allsorted Ltd WD19 4BG U.K.

The publisher is not responsible for the outcome of any recipe you try from this book. You may not achieve the results desired due to variations in ingredients, typos, errors, omissions, or individual ability. You should always take care not to injure yourself or others on sharp knives or other cooking implements or to burn yourself or others while cooking. You should examine the contents of ingredients prior to preparation and consumption of these recipes in order to be fully aware of and to accurately advise others of the presence of substances which might provoke an adverse reaction in some consumers. Recipes in this book may not have been formally tested by us or for us and we do not provide any assurances nor accept any responsibility or liability with regard to their originality, efficacy, quality or safety.

This book contains information that may fall out of date and is intended only to education and entertain.

The publisher shall have no liability or responsibility to any person or entity regarding any loss or damage incurred or alleged to have occurred directly, or indirectly, by the information contained within this book.

This book is intended for adults only. Please drink responsibly.

All rights reserved. No part of this work may be reproduced in any form or by any means, electronic or mechanical, including photocopying, recording or by any information storage and retrieval system, without the prior written permission of the publisher.

© Susanna Geoghegan Gift Publishing

Author: Helen Vaux
Cover and concept design: Milestone Creative
Contents design: seagulls.net

ISBN 9781915902641

Printed in China

10 9 8 7 6 5 4 3 2 1

CONTENTS

Introduction 5

All about gin 6

Gin tasting tips 10

Tools and glasses 12

Techniques and terms 16

Infusing your own gin 18

Drinks and cocktails 20

Cooking with gin 136

Other uses for gin 154

Gin quotes 158

'The only day I ever enjoyed ironing
was the day I accidentally got
gin in the steam iron.'

Phyllis Diller

INTRODUCTION

Gin has captivated people's palates for centuries. With its distinctive flavour derived from juniper berries, it has become the foundation of many classic and contemporary drinks and cocktails. But that isn't it's only use – gin has been used in cooking, beauty products, aftershave, soap and even chocolate.

Peruse the range of gins in your local store these days and you'll be spoilt for choice. Flavoured gin, pink gin, sloe gin, dry gin, Old Tom, navy strength ... where to start? Don't feel overwhelmed – the fun is in discovering what you like and what makes your tastebuds tingle. One thing's for sure – you'll never get bored!

Whether you're a gin connoisseur or a curious newcomer, this book shows you how versatile gin can be. It explores the many aspects that gin has to offer which contribute to its unique character. There's far more to say about this unique liquid than we can fit in this book, but hopefully, it will give you a taster (literally!) of the wonderful world of gin.

ALL ABOUT GIN

WHAT IS GIN?

Gin is a distilled alcoholic drink that takes its primary flavour from juniper berries. The berries have a fruity citrus flavour alongside an an aromatic, piney spiciness. Different gins are made using a range of 'botanicals' that give them their distinct flavour in addition to the juniper berries. Botanicals can be fruits, herbs and spices or other plant materials. This means that no two brands of gin are alike.

A BRIEF HISTORY OF GIN

Gin originated as a medicinal liquor made by monks across Europe. Modern gin, as we know it, arrived from Belgium and the Netherlands in the form of jenever (or 'Dutch gin') and became hugely popular in England. Gin became even more popular after the 1688 Glorious Revolution, when import restrictions were placed on French brandy.

The first half of the 18th century saw the height of the Gin Craze in Britain, particularly in London. For the working classes, gin kept them warm, staved off hunger and provided an escape from the misery of life in the slums. Gin became known as 'Mother's Ruin' and drunkenness and addiction were commonplace.

In 1730, there were 7,000 gin shops in London, and that's not counting the rest of the country! In the 19th century, gin shops started to be replaced by 'gin palaces'. These were slightly more glamorous destinations where one could simply buy a shot of gin and leave.

By the second half of the 19th century, gin became increasingly popular as a cocktail ingredient. It reached the height of fashion in the 1920s and became THE spirit everyone talked about. In fact, there are more classic cocktails made with gin than any other spirit.

Gin has had a huge renaissance in the 21st century. Flavoured gins are proving ever popular and since 2017, over 200 new gins have entered the market in the UK. Demand has hit an all-time high and doesn't show signs of slowing. If you love gin, this is your time!

STYLES OF GIN

London Dry – The most familiar and common gin style, dating back to the early 19th century. All the flavour ingredients are extracted before or during distillation. There is no sweetness in a London Dry.

Contemporary / New World – Uses lots of botanicals in addition to juniper and is usually sweeter than London Dry.

Plymouth – Drier and more citrusy than London Dry and has an earthy flavour.

ALL ABOUT GIN

Old Tom – A richer and sweeter gin than London Dry.

Navy Strength – In the 18th century, the British navy stored their gin below decks near the gunpowder. If any gin leaked, the gunpowder would still ignite if the gins were over 100 proof (hence 'Navy Strength'). The name applies to gin over 57% ABV.

Genever – Created in 16th-century Holland, this gin is made with malted grains and the alcohol content is lower than other styles of gin (35%). 'Genever' is also the Dutch word for juniper.

HOW IS GIN MADE?

The process for making gin begins with a neutral grain or base spirit to which botanicals are added. These botanicals, including juniper berries, are infused during the distillation or post-distillation process to create the flavour of the gin.

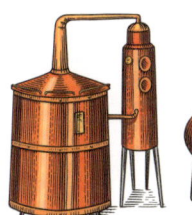

The mixture is then distilled. This lets the alcohol vapour interact with the botanicals and extract their essences. Finally, the gin is diluted and bottled. It will sometimes be aged, depending on the flavour the maker wants to achieve.

FASCINATING GIN FACTS

The country with the world's highest per capita gin consumption is the Philippines.

Juniper berries aren't actually berries. They are seed cones – like a pinecone – and only have the appearance of a berry.

English soldiers fighting in the Thirty Years War in the Netherlands during the 17th century called jenever 'Dutch Courage' because it helped to steel them for battle. Hence the saying.

World Gin Day is observed annually on the second Saturday of June. Originating in 2009, celebratory events now take place on this day in over 30 countries.

GIN TASTING TIPS

GIN TASTING TIPS

HOW TO TASTE GIN

1. USE THE BEST GLASS FOR TASTING

Choosing the right glass can really help you appreciate gin's flavours. A tulip-shaped glass, such as a small to medium-sized wine glass, is the best option as it concentrates the aromas.

2. LOOK BEFORE YOU SIP

Have a look at the gin's appearance by holding it up to the light. How clear is it? What colour is it? Gin tends to be clear, but some have a slight colour depending on their age or ingredients. The clearer a gin is, the higher quality the distillation process it has been through.

3. TAKE IT FOR A SWIRL

Gently swirl the gin in your glass. This helps enhance the aromas.

4. INHALE!

Put your nose in the glass and inhale slowly. What aromas can you detect? For example, it might smell floral, citrusy or spicy, or a combination of these.

5. HAVE A SIP

Take a small sip to enjoy the gin's base flavours, including the juniper and any botanicals. Is it sweet, bitter or acidic? What is the texture like? It might be smooth or it could be slightly oily. (It depends on how the gin has been made.)

6. SWALLOW

After you swallow, what taste lingers? (This is the 'finish'.) You might even notice some new flavours that you didn't detect before.

TOOLS & GLASSES

TOOLS & GLASSES

Most cocktails and mixed drinks are easy to make. You won't need any fancy gadgets to create the recipes in this book. However, it does help to have a few essential tools to hand. These will make your life easier and ensure you get the best out of the recipe.

THE BASICS

Jigger: Precision is key when you're mixing drinks. A jigger will ensure you measure all your ingredients precisely and get the right balance of flavours.

Cocktail shaker: For shaking at home, a traditional Cobbler shaker is all you need. It consists of a metal container, cap and a built-in strainer.

Strainer: Even if your shaker has a built-in strainer, some recipes require you to 'double strain' the drink to make it as smooth as possible. A strainer is simply placed on top of the glass as you pour in the drink. A Hawthorne strainer is specifically used for fine straining.

Muddler: A muddle looks a bit like a long, thin pestle and pretty much does the same job. See 'Muddling' on page 16.

GLASSES

Cocktail etiquette demands a particular glass for a particular drink. To be honest, you don't need to follow the rules at home! (Unless, of course, you have endless cupboard space.) These are the glasses mentioned in this book:

Balloon – Generous bowl for cocktails over ice.

Champagne flute – Long-stemmed with an elongated, slender bowl.

Collins – Tall and slender, ideal for serving long drinks.

Coupe – A stemmed glass with a fairly round, shallow bowl with straight sides, unlike the V-shape of a martini glass.

Highball – Ideal for long, tall drinks. (Not as tall as a Collins glass but generally interchangeable.)

Lowball/Rocks/Old Fashioned – A short tumbler.

Martini – A long-stemmed, V-shaped glass with a wide rim.

Mixing glass – If you're not shaking a cocktail, you may need a mixing glass. Basically, this is a generously sturdy glass, often with a handy pouring spout.

Nick & Nora – A long-stemmed, high-sided inverted bowl shape with a narrow rim.

TECHNIQUES & TERMS

Cocktail bartenders are known for their coolness and flamboyance. Don't worry though, no one expects you to hippy hippy shake like Tom Cruise in *Cocktail*. If you're a beginner, just focus on getting the measures right, shaking for long enough and not spilling the drink!

As an amateur mixologist working in the confines of your own home (and probably without an audience), what are the techniques and terms that you need to know? Here are the key ones you'll come across in this book:

Dash – As careless as a dash sounds, in the cocktail world it's quite precise and is the equivalent of 0.9ml or 12 drops. Realistically, an extra drop or two isn't the end of the world.

Straining – Traditional cocktail shakers have built-in strainers – the part that sits in the top of the shaker with holes in it. Straining gets rid of any unwanted bits in your drink as you pour it into the glass. It also stops the ice you shake with from tipping into your glass. Sometimes a cocktail requires 'double straining' – basically, passing it through a strainer twice (or through two strainers put together).

Muddling – This technique requires a muddler (see page 13). Muddling gently 'bruises' a fresh ingredient (for example mint leaves or fruit segments) so that they release their flavours into the drink. Be careful not to 'over muddle' herbs as this can introduce unwanted bitterness.

TECHNIQUE & TERMS

Shaking – Using a cocktail shaker doesn't simply mix the ingredients, it also chills them. When you've added the ingredients and ice, hold the shaker in both hands – one hand on top and the other on the base – and give it a sharp shake. When waters begin to condense on the outside of the shaker, it means that the cocktail inside is chilled.

Dry shaking – As 'Shaking' above, but you don't put ice in the shaker. This is usually used when a recipe contains egg whites. Dry shaking allow the proteins of the whites to coagulate, aerate and create a foam.

Stirring – The best and most effective way to stir a cocktail is with a bar spoon, or a metal or wooden stick. It's a gentler way to combine ingredients than shaking. Make your stirring slow, steady and smooth. If there's ice in the glass, stirring also helps to melt the ice and slightly dilute the drink.

Simple syrup – For adding sweetness to cocktails. Simply dissolve 300g of caster sugar in 150ml of water in a saucepan over a low heat. Leave to cool and then bottle. Store in the fridge.

INFUSING YOUR OWN GIN

INFUSING YOUR OWN GIN

Gin comes in lots of different flavours and buying a decent one can be expensive. The good news is that it's incredibly easy to infuse your own gin. The benefits of doing it yourself are that you can choose your favourite flavours and try combinations you might not find in the shops. Variety is the spice of life, after all!

To make your flavoured gin, start with a dry, sterilised jar or bottle with an airtight lid. Add your chosen fruit, herbs and/or spices and then top the jar up with a good quality, everyday gin.

The general rule is to use two-thirds gin and one-third fruit/herbs/spices. Only add small quantities of any ingredients that are particularly potent, such as chilli peppers!

The longer you leave it to infuse, the stronger your gin's flavours will be. Herbs and spices may only need a few hours, whereas fruits, vegetables and berries might need one to two weeks (or a little longer). Taste the gin every so often until you're happy with the flavour and avoid leaving it for too long.

When you're happy with the result, strain the gin into a clean, dry bottle using a muslin cloth to filter out the additional ingredients. If kept in a cool, dark place with the lid sealed, your gin should last for several months.

Suggested flavourings: Rhubarb; ginger; orange; raspberries; rosemary; thyme; lavender; mint; celery; vanilla; chilli; caramel; plums; peaches. See also the recipe for Sloe Gin on page 114.

DRINKS & COCKTAILS

DRINKS & COCKTAILS

Akaibara Cooler 22
Aviation 24
Bee's Knees 26
Bijou 28
Bittersweet Symphony 30
Bluebird 32
Boxcar 34
Bramble 36
Bronx 38
Casino 40
Classic G&T 42
Classic Martini 44
Clover Club 46
Corpse Reviver No. 2 48
Diabola 50
Dubonnet & Gin 52
Earl Grey Martini 54
Elderflower Collin 56
Espresso Gin Martini 58
Feisty Charlotte 60
Fog Cutter 62
French 75 64
Garden Game 66
Gibson 68
Gimlet 70
Gin Basil Smash 72
Gin Fizz 74
Ginger Gin Mule 76
Gin Rickey 78
Grapefruit, Rosemary & Gin 80
Greyhound 82
Hanky Panky 84
Honolulu 86
Hot Gin Toddy 88
Hugo 90
Juliet & Romeo 92
Long Island Iced Tea 94
Monkey Gland 96
Mince Pie Martini 98
Mulled Gin 100
Negroni 102
Pink Negroni 104
Ramos Gin Fizz 106
Red Snapper 108
Singapore Sling 110
Slippery When Wet 112
Sloe Gin 114
Southside 116
Sublime Moment 118
Sugar & Spice & Everything Nice 120
The Gardener's Daughter 120
The Last Word 120
Tom Collins 120
Tropical Stranger 120
Vesper Martini 130
White Lady 132
White Rabbit 134

THE LITTLE BOOK OF GIN

AKAIBARA COOLER

AKAIBARA COOLER

SERVES: 1 | SERVED IN: HIGHBALL GLASS

Love pink? Love summer? Then this is the cocktail for you. Floral and refreshing, this rose-tinted drink is a sure-fire winner whether you're throwing a party with friends or simply kicking back in your garden on a warm, sunny day.

YOU WILL NEED

30ml gin

15ml rose vermouth

10ml rose petal liqueur

100ml pink lemonade

Strawberries or raspberries, to garnish

METHOD

1. Fill a highball glass with ice. Pour in the gin, vermouth and rose petal liqueur. Stir.
2. Top up the glass with the pink lemonade. Garnish with the red berries.

BARTENDER TIP

Watermelon goes brilliantly with gin. For an extra splash of summer, add a dash of watermelon juice to your gin cocktail and garnish with a slice of fresh watermelon.

AVIATION

SERVES: 1 | SERVED IN: COUPE OR MARTINI GLASS

This classic violet-coloured cocktail was invented in New York and is the perfect aperitif. The sourness of the lemon is balanced out by the sweet cherry liqueur. The name comes from the world's obsession with anything aeronautical in the early 1900s.

YOU WILL NEED

60ml gin

7.5ml Crème de Violette or Creme Yvette

15ml maraschino liqueur

22.5ml lemon juice

Maraschino cherry to garnish

METHOD

1. Add the ingredients into a cocktail shaker filled with ice. Shake well to mix thoroughly.
2. Strain into the glass.
3. To garnish, drop in the cherry.

BARTENDER TIP

Invest in proper maraschino cherries. The red cocktail cherries you find on ice cream sundaes lack both flavour and sophistication! Failing that, fresh cherries are the next best option.

THE LITTLE BOOK OF GIN

AVIATION

THE LITTLE BOOK OF GIN

BEE'S KNEES

BEE'S KNEES

SERVES: 1 | SERVED IN: COUPE GLASS

Made with gin, lemon and honey, this cocktail is strong, refreshing and delicious. Choose a milder flavoured honey so that it doesn't overpower the gin. The lemon juice complements both the sweetness of the honey and the tartness of the gin.

YOU WILL NEED

60ml gin

22.5ml lemon juice, freshly squeezed

15ml honey syrup (see Bartender Tip below)

Lemon twist, to garnish

METHOD

1. Fill a cocktail shaker with ice and add the gin, lemon juice and honey syrup. Shake until thoroughly chilled.
2. Strain into a chilled glass.
3. Garnish with a lemon twist.

BARTENDER TIP

To make honey syrup, combine 120ml of honey and 120ml of water in a saucepan. Stir over a medium heat until the honey dissolves. Allow to cool and transfer to an airtight container. Keep refrigerated for up to one month.

BIJOU

SERVES: 1 | SERVED IN: COUPE GLASS

The Bijou was created by the father of bartending, Harry Johnson, who named it after the colours of three jewels: chartreuse for emeralds, vermouth for rubies and gin for diamonds. It's a sophisticated cocktail with complex sweet, herbal flavours.

YOU WILL NEED

30ml gin

30ml sweet vermouth

30ml green Chartreuse

1 dash orange bitters

Lemon peel, to garnish

METHOD

1. Fill a mixing glass with ice and pour in the ingredients. Stir well to combine.
2. Strain into a chilled glass.
3. Garnish with a twist of lemon peel.

BARTENDER TIP

'The greatest accomplishment of a bartender lies in his ability to exactly suit his customer.'

Harry Johnson

THE LITTLE BOOK OF GIN

BIJOU

THE LITTLE BOOK OF GIN

BITTERSWEET SYMPHONY

BITTERSWEET SYMPHONY

SERVES: 1 | SERVED IN: NICK & NORA GLASS

This drink does exactly what it says on the tin and provides a symphony of taste sensations. Aperol has the flavour of sweet oranges and bittersweet citrus notes. Add to that Punt e Mes, a sweet vermouth with bitter, herbal tones.

YOU WILL NEED

45ml gin

22.5ml Punt e Mes

22.5ml Aperol

Lemon or lime slice, to garnish

METHOD

1. Add all the ingredients (apart from the garnish) to a cocktail shaker with a handful of ice.
2. Stir all the ingredients together.
3. Strain into a chilled glass.
4. Garnish with the lemon or lime slice and serve.

BARTENDER TIP

When mixing cocktails for a group, batching ingredients will improve your efficiency! For example, you can pre-mix all the ingredients for a Negroni and store it in the fridge until you're ready to serve.

BLUEBIRD

SERVES: 1 | SERVED IN: COUPE OR MARTINI GLASS

This Bluebird's stunning colour comes from the blue curaçao. It's both sweet and tart in flavour – play around with the proportions to find what suits you. To make it less sweet, cut back on the curaçao. If you prefer extra tartness, simply add more lemon juice. Then take flight and enjoy!

YOU WILL NEED

- 45ml gin
- 22.5ml blue curaçao
- 15ml fresh lemon juice
- 1-2 dashes aromatic bitters
- Lemon peel, to garnish

METHOD

1. Add the gin, blue curaçao, lemon juice and bitters to a cocktail shaker filled with ice.
2. Shake until the shaker is cold to touch.
3. Strain into a chilled glass.
3. Garnish with a twist of lemon peel and serve.

BARTENDER TIP

To make a lemon twist garnish, simply cut a round slice from the thickest part of the lemon and make one cut from the edge to the middle. Remove the flesh and pith from the peel. Twist the peel into a 'spring' shape.

THE LITTLE BOOK OF GIN

BLUEBIRD

THE LITTLE BOOK OF GIN

BOXCAR

BOXCAR

SERVES: 1 | SERVED IN: COUPE GLASS

The Boxcar is a well-rounded, sour gin cocktail that was popular in the 1940s. A splash of grenadine gives this drink its lovely pale pink colour and extra sweetness. (You can leave the grenadine out if you prefer your gin cocktails a little drier.)

YOU WILL NEED

45 ml gin	2 tbsp sugar
15ml Cointreau	Lemon wedge
20ml fresh lemon juice	1 egg white
5ml Grenadine	

METHOD

1. Rub the rim of the glass with a wedge of a lemon and then dip in the sugar.
2. Add all the ingredients to a cocktail shaker. Dry shake (without ice) for 1-2 minutes.
3. Add a handful of ice and shake for a further minute.
4. Strain into a chilled glass.

BARTENDER TIP

For a less sugary drink, swap the Cointreau in the recipe for Grand Marnier.

BRAMBLE

SERVES: 1 | SERVED IN: ROCKS OR OLD FASHIONED GLASS

The bartender who named the Bramble was inspired by his memories of blackberry picking as a child on the Isle of Wight. With the crushed ice, you'll enjoy a thoroughly adult slushie! Turn your Bramble into a Bramble Royale by topping up the glass with champagne.

YOU WILL NEED

50ml gin

30ml fresh lemon juice

15ml simple syrup (see page 17)

15ml blackberry liqueur (e.g. Crème de Mûre)

Lemon slice or blackberries, to garnish

METHOD

1. Fill a cocktail shaker with ice. Add the gin, lemon juice and simple syrup. Shake until the shaker is cold to touch.
2. Fill a small tumbler with crushed ice and pour over the shaken mixture. Drizzle the blackberry liqueur over the top so that it slowly drains down into the glass.
3. Garnish with a lemon slice or blackberries.

BARTENDER TIP

To make crushed ice, place ice cubes in a clean tea towel or sealable bag and gently crush with a blunt kitchen utensil, for example a rolling pin. Do this just before you need the ice as it will melt more quickly than ice cubes.

THE LITTLE BOOK OF GIN

BRAMBLE

THE LITTLE BOOK OF GIN

BRONX

BRONX

SERVES: 1 | SERVED IN: COUPE GLASS

Mildly sweet, without being sticky, legend has it that the Bronx was the first cocktail to use fruit juice. It was created in the early 1900s at the Waldorf-Astoria hotel in New York and was named after the newly opened Bronx Zoo.

YOU WILL NEED

45ml gin

22.5ml fresh orange juice

22.5ml dry vermouth

22.5ml sweet vermouth

Orange slice, to garnish

METHOD

1. Fill a cocktail shaker with ice and add all the ingredients. Shake well for 10 seconds.
2. Strain into a chilled glass.
3. Garnish with an orange slice.

BARTENDER TIP

Replace plain orange juice with blood orange juice to create a Bloody Bronx. You can also add a dash of Angostura bitters for an extra zing.

CASINO

SERVES: 1 | SERVED IN: COUPE GLASS

The stakes are high with this sophisticated cocktail. The zesty lemon juice complements the botanicals in the gin, while the maraschino liqueur delivers a fruity pop of cherry. Finally, there's the orange bitters – they might be subtle but they add an exciting twist.

YOU WILL NEED

40ml gin

10ml fresh lemon juice

10ml orange bitters

10ml Maraschino cherry liqueur

Lemon twist or maraschino cherry, to garnish

METHOD

1. Add all ingredients to a cocktail shaker with ice.
2. Shake vigorously until the shaker is cold to touch.
3. Strain into a chilled glass.
4. Garnish with a lemon twist or a maraschino cherry. Serve.

BARTENDER TIP

If you'd prefer your Casino cocktail to be sweeter, slightly increase the amount of maraschino liqueur.

THE LITTLE BOOK OF GIN

CASINO

THE LITTLE BOOK OF GIN

CLASSIC G&T

CLASSIC G&T

SERVES: 1 | SERVED IN: HIGHBALL GLASS

The G&T was invented in the early 1800s by the British Army as the quinine in the tonic water helped prevent malaria. It's simple to make, yet there's still an art to perfecting the humble G&T. A perfect balance of bitter and sweet, the tonic brings out all the flavour components of the gin and boosts the botanicals.

YOU WILL NEED

50ml gin

Tonic water (chilled)

Wedge of lime

METHOD

1. Fill a chilled highball glass with ice cubes.
2. Pour the gin over the ice and top up with the tonic water.
3. Gently squeeze a wedge of lime into the glass and then drop it in. Stir gently.

BARTENDER TIP

For the ultimate G&T, keep your ingredients (including the gin) as cold as possible and use minimal garnishes. The slower you pour in the tonic, the more bubbles you'll have, making your G&T crisper.

CLASSIC MARTINI

SERVES: 1 | SERVED IN: MARTINI GLASS

Thought to have originated in the 1860s, this is probably the most famous and iconic gin cocktail of all. It's elegant, sharp and dry. The 'drier' you want your martini, the less vermouth you add. Experiment to see what suits your tastebuds best. A martini can also be served over ice in an old fashioned glass.

YOU WILL NEED

| 50ml gin | Zest of a lemon |
| 15ml dry vermouth | A couple of green olives |

METHOD

1. Pour the gin and dry vermouth into a cocktail shaker with ice. Stir well – don't shake – treating it gently will prevent it from clouding.

2. Strain into a chilled martini glass, ideally one that has been in the freezer.

3. Peel off a strip of lemon zest and twist it into a spiral. Hang on the side of the glass. Finally, put your olives on a cocktail stick and float them in the glass.

BARTENDER TIP

A martini can also be made with vodka in place of gin. In fact, it was vodka martinis that James Bond would famously order 'shaken not stirred'.

THE LITTLE BOOK OF GIN

CLASSIC MARTINI

THE LITTLE BOOK OF GIN

CLOVER CLUB

CLOVER CLUB

SERVES: 1 | SERVED IN: COUPE GLASS

This sweet and creamy raspberry-flavoured cocktail was first made at the bar of a hotel in Philadelphia at the turn of the 20th century. It takes its name from a men's social club that met at the US hotel between the 1880s and 1920s, before Prohibition.

YOU WILL NEED

60ml gin

22.5ml fresh lemon juice

22.5ml raspberry syrup

1 egg white

Raspberries, to garnish

METHOD

1. Dry shake (without ice) the egg white in an empty cocktail shaker for 15 seconds.
2. Add the remaining ingredients and shake again.
3. Strain into a chilled glass.
4. Garnish with raspberries skewered on a cocktail stick.

BARTENDER TIP

Swap the raspberry syrup with grenadine for a slightly different flavour but same berry colour. Or use vermouth to add a light bitter taste.

CORPSE REVIVER NO. 2

SERVES: 1 | SERVED IN: COUPE OR MARTINI GLASS

The name alone makes this the perfect cocktail to serve at an adults' Halloween party. Unlike its brandy-based sibling – the Corpse Reviver No. 1 – the No. 2 is a fresher, and more tart, citrussy option. As the name suggests, these cocktails were created to supposedly relieve hangovers!

YOU WILL NEED

- 25ml gin
- 25ml white wine-based aperitif (such as Lillet Blanc)
- 25ml triple sec
- 25ml lemon juice
- 5ml absinthe
- 5ml simple syrup (see page 17)
- Orange peel, to garnish

METHOD

1. Put a large handful of ice in a cocktail shaker. Add all the ingredients (apart from the orange peel). Shake until the outside of the shaker is cold to touch.
2. Strain into a glass.
3. Garnish with a strip of orange peel.

BARTENDER TIP

If you find this drink a little too sour, simply reduce the amount of lemon juice and add an extra 5ml (1 tsp) of simple syrup.

THE LITTLE BOOK OF GIN

CORPSE REVIVER NO. 2

THE LITTLE BOOK OF GIN

DIABOLA

DIABOLA

SERVES: 1 | SERVED IN: COUPE GLASS

In Latin, the word 'diabola' means the 'evil one', so it's perfect if you're looking for a cocktail that's easy to make and tastes devilishly good. Dubonnet is a sweet, fortified wine with hints of chocolate and raspberries, and a refreshing bitterness. The orgeat syrup adds a delicious nuttiness to this rich cocktail.

YOU WILL NEED

40ml Dubonnet

20ml gin

2 dashes orgeat syrup (made with almonds, not suitable if you have a nut allergy)

METHOD

1. Fill a cocktail shaker with ice and add all the ingredients. Shake well.
2. Strain into a chilled glass.

BARTENDER TIP

Because of the high Dubonnet to gin ratio in this drink, use a bold, strong-flavoured gin to allow its flavour to shine through a little more.

DUBONNET AND GIN

SERVES: 1 | SERVED IN: COUPE OR SMALL WINE GLASS

A Dubonnet and Gin was the favourite aperitif of the late Queen Elizabeth II – it is said that she would have one every day before lunch. Dubonnet is made from a blend of fortified wine infused with herbs and spices, including blackcurrant and black tea. This is a dry drink with tons of flavour.

YOU WILL NEED

30ml gin

60ml Dubonnet Rouge

Lemon or orange wheels, to garnish

METHOD

1. Add the gin and Dubonnet to a cocktail shaker or mixing glass along with a handful of ice. Stir well.
2. Strain into a chilled glass.
3. Drop the lemon or orange wheel in. Serve (with or without ice).

BARTENDER TIP

All bartenders know that being organised is the key to making great drinks. Read the recipe first and have all the ingredients and equipment you need to hand before you begin pouring.

THE LITTLE BOOK OF GIN

DUBONNET AND GIN

THE LITTLE BOOK OF GIN

EARL GREY MARTINI

EARL GREY MARTINI

SERVES: 1 | SERVED IN: MARTINI GLASS (OR A TEACUP!)

Tea doesn't need to be hot and from a teapot. Try this for a fabulous twist on a gin martini – bergamot oil in the Earl Grey provides a wonderful citrus hit. It's an elegant cocktail guaranteed to make you feel sophisticated.

YOU WILL NEED

50ml gin

35ml strong Earl Grey tea (cold)

20ml lemon juice

12.5ml simple syrup (see recipe on page 17)

½ egg white

Lemon peel, to garnish

METHOD

1. Add the gin, Earl Grey tea, lemon juice, simple syrup and egg white to a cocktail shaker. Dry shake (without ice) well for 10-15 seconds.
2. Add ice to the shaker and shake again until cold.
3. Strain into a martini glass.
4. Garnish by dropping in a piece of lemon peel.

BARTENDER TIP

Both stages of shaking are important. The first – the 'dry shake' - will help to emulsify the egg white and create a gorgeous silky texture.

ELDERFLOWER COLLINS

SERVES: 1 | SERVED IN: COLLINS GLASS

Cool and refreshing, the Elderflower Collins combines delicate floral and fruity flavours. The lemon juice works perfectly to balance out the flavours. Ideal for balmy summer evenings as you watch the sun go down.

YOU WILL NEED

60ml gin

30ml fresh lemon juice

15ml elderflower cordial

125ml soda water, to taste

Slice of lemon, to garnish

METHOD

1. Fill a cocktail shaker with ice. Add the gin, lemon juice and elderflower cordial. Shake vigorously for 10 seconds.
2. Double strain into a glass with fresh ice.
3. Top up the glass with soda water. Gently stir.
4. Garnish with the lemon slice and serve.

BARTENDER TIP

Swapping the gin for pink gin is a great way to make this drink look even more special – especially if you're serving it on Valentine's Day!

THE LITTLE BOOK OF GIN

ELDERFLOWER COLLINS

THE LITTLE BOOK OF GIN

ESPRESSO GIN MARTINI

ESPRESSO GIN MARTINI

SERVES: 1 | SERVED IN: MARTINI GLASS

The espresso gin martini is a twist on the classic cocktail. If you like Irish coffee, you'll find this smooth, strong and delicious. It's a fantastic after dinner cocktail.

YOU WILL NEED

45ml gin

45ml Kahlúa

30ml espresso

15ml simple syrup (see page 17)

Coffee beans, to garnish

METHOD

1. Make an espresso and leave to cool completely.
2. Add the gin, Kahlúa, espresso, simple syrup and a handful of ice cubes to a cocktail shaker.
3. Shake vigorously for 30 seconds.
4. Strain into a chilled glass quickly – do it quickly to create the foam!
5. Garnish with coffee beans. Serve.

BARTENDER TIP

Don't be impatient. Make sure the espresso is cooled completely before you use it. If it's still warm, the ice will melt and you'll end up with a diluted, watery cocktail.

FIESTY CHARLOTTE

SERVES: 1 | SERVED IN: COUPE GLASS

The liqueurs are what make this feisty cocktail with a touch of floral sweetness special. Galliano is an Italian sweet herbal liqueur with a vanilla/anise flavour and subtle citrus tones. Suze is a traditional French aperitif *liqueur* flavoured with gentian root, making it spicy, fruity and slightly bitter.

YOU WILL NEED

60ml gin	60ml tangerine juice
60ml Galliano liqueur	1 egg
30ml Suze liqueur	30ml fresh lemon juice
30ml elderflower syrup	Edible flowers, to garnish

METHOD

1. Add all the ingredients (except for the garnish) to a cocktail shaker. Dry shake (without ice) thoroughly for around two minutes until the egg white becomes frothy.

2. Add a handful of ice to the cocktail shaker. Shake until the shaker is cold to touch.

3. Strain into a glass.

4. Garnish with flowers and serve.

BARTENDER TIP

Orange and grapefruit juice are suitable replacements for tangerine juice. Yes, the taste will be slightly different but the overall combination of flavours and undertones will be just as good.

THE LITTLE BOOK OF GIN

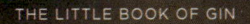

FIESTY
CHARLOTTE

THE LITTLE BOOK OF GIN

FOG CUTTER

FOG CUTTER

SERVES: 1 | SERVED IN: HIGHBALL GLASS OR TIKI MUG

The Fog Cutter is a vintage tiki cocktail, a category of cocktails that are usually made with rum and are often colourful and fruity. This one tastes great, but it also looks fantastic if you can successfully 'float' the sherry on top of the drink. A steady hand is required – good luck!

YOU WILL NEED

40ml light rum

20ml cognac

20ml gin

30ml fresh lime juice

30ml orange juice

15ml orgeat syrup (made with almonds, not suitable if you have a nut allergy)

10ml cream sherry

Mint sprigs or cocktail cherry, to garnish

METHOD

1. Place all the ingredients (apart from the sherry and garnishes) into a cocktail shaker. Shake for 15-30 seconds.

2. Strain into a glass and top with crushed ice (see Bartender Tip on page 37).

3. Slowly pour the sherry over the crushed ice so that it floats on the top of the drink.

4. Garnish with mint sprigs or a cocktail cherry.

BARTENDER TIP

The orgeat syrup doesn't contain alcohol but adds a taste of almond to the Fog Cutter. The syrup pairs well with brandy and whiskey, as well as rum.

FRENCH 75

SERVES: 1 | SERVED IN: CHAMPAGNE FLUTE

Although this is a simple and elegant cocktail, its name is said to refer to the 75mm Howitzer field gun used by French and American troops in the First World War. The 'kick' delivered by the French 75 cocktail was said to feel like being hit by the weapon!

YOU WILL NEED

45ml gin

15ml lemon juice

7.5ml simple syrup

Champagne, chilled

Lemon peel, to garnish

METHOD

1. Fill a cocktail shaker with ice and add the gin, lemon juice and simple syrup. Shake well to combine.
2. Strain into a glass and then top up with the champagne.
3. Garnish with piece of lemon peel.

BARTENDER TIP

You can replace the champagne with prosecco or sparkling wine; however, to get the best results, it's worth investing in a good bottle of champagne.

THE LITTLE BOOK OF GIN

FRENCH 75

THE LITTLE BOOK OF GIN

GARDEN
GAME

GARDEN GAME

SERVES: 1 | SERVED IN: COUPE OR MARTINI GLASS

This drink has fruitiness in spades, yet the 'garden' in this 'game' also embraces the earthiness of the great outdoors. Combining herbs from your garden (or windowsill) with the gin adds a refreshingly herby bite. This a cocktail to sip after a hard day of planting and pruning.

YOU WILL NEED

50ml gin

40ml pineapple juice

15ml fresh lemon juice

15ml peach liqueur

Sprig of lemon thyme, to garnish

METHOD

1. Pour all the ingredients into a cocktail shaker and fill with ice.
2. Shake for 15-20 seconds or until the shaker is cold to touch.
3. Double strain into a chilled glass.
4. Garnish with the lemon thyme.

BARTENDER TIP

If you don't like lemon thyme, experiment with any other herb, such as tarragon or rosemary.

GIBSON

SERVES: 1 | SERVED IN: COUPE OR MARTINI GLASS

The main difference between a Gibson and a classic gin martini is simply the garnish. Rather than an olive, a Gibson is garnished with a pickled cocktail onion. It doesn't sound like much of a difference, but the onions provide a very different underlying flavour.

YOU WILL NEED

3 small pickled cocktail onions

60ml gin

12.5ml dry vermouth

METHOD

1. Pour the gin and vermouth into a jug or mixing glass. Add a handful of ice and stir for 30 seconds.
2. Strain into a chilled glass.
3. Drop in the pickled onions and serve.

BARTENDER TIP

Did you know that it's traditional to use either one or three cocktail onions in a Gibson? There's an old superstition among bar tenders that an even number of onions (or olives) is bad luck.

THE LITTLE BOOK OF GIN

GIBSON

THE LITTLE BOOK OF GIN

GIMLET

GIMLET

SERVES: 1 | SERVED IN: COUPE OR MARTINI GLASS

In the 19th century, the Royal Navy used to mix gin with lime cordial to prevent scurvy. Scurvy was common on long voyages and was caused by not consuming enough vitamin C. This seafaring self-medication became a cocktail known as the Gimlet.

YOU WILL NEED

50ml gin

50ml Rose's lime cordial

Slice of lime, to garnish

METHOD

1. Put all your ingredients in a shaker filled with ice.
2. Shake well and then strain into a chilled glass.
3. Garnish with a slice of lime.

BARTENDER TIP

Make sure you shake your cocktails for long enough. A useful rule of thumb is to shake it until your cocktail shaker is so cold, it's painful to touch!

GIN BASIL SMASH

SERVES: 1 | SERVED IN: ROCKS OR OLD FASHIONED GLASS

A refreshing, herby cocktail that's perfect for summer. It's incredibly easy to make but that doesn't make it any less impressive – either for your guests or your tastebuds. Enjoy the combination of sweet, sour and bitter notes, complemented by the tang of lemon.

YOU WILL NEED

50ml gin

25ml fresh lemon juice

15ml simple syrup (see page 17)

1 bunch of basil leaves (reserve some to garnish)

METHOD

1. Put the basil and lemon into a cocktail shaker. Gently muddle the lemon and basil to 'smash' them.
2. Add simple syrup and gin and then top up the shaker with ice. Shake vigorously until the shaker feels cold to touch.
3. Double strain into an ice-filled rocks glass.
4. Garnish with basil leaves to serve.

BARTENDER TIP

If you want a fresher – and less herbal – gin smash, don't muddle the basil. Simply add all the ingredients to the cocktail shaker, shake, strain and serve.

THE LITTLE BOOK OF GIN

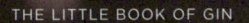

GIN BASIL SMASH

THE LITTLE BOOK OF GIN

GIN FIZZ

GIN FIZZ

SERVES: 1 | SERVED IN: HIGHBALL GLASS

The Gin Fizz comes from the very beginnings of cocktail history. Originating in the 19th century, it's a sour-based, incredibly refreshing cocktail. The traditional recipe includes an egg white, but it is equally delicious – and less frothy – without it.

YOU WILL NEED

60ml gin

30ml lemon juice

20ml simple syrup

120ml soda water

1 lemon wedge

METHOD

1. Pour the gin, lemon juice and simple syrup into an ice-filled cocktail shaker. Shake well.
2. Strain into the glass and the add the soda water.
3. Garnish with a lemon wedge. Don't serve with ice – it's not meant to be diluted!

BARTENDER TIP

Turn up the glamour! Substitute champagne for the soda water to create a Diamond Fizz.

GINGER GIN MULE

SERVES: 1 | SERVED IN: COPPER MUG

Gin and ginger is a spicy combination and this refreshing drink delivers a delicious, crisp punch. With tangy lime juice and cooling mint, a Ginger Gin Mule is a great go-to drink for a sunny evening in the garden.

YOU WILL NEED

60ml gin

30ml fresh lime juice

Ginger beer

Fresh mint, to garnish

Lime wedges, to garnish

METHOD

1. Add the gin and lime juice to a cocktail shaker. Fill the shaker with ice. Shake vigorously until the shaker is cold to the touch.
2. Strain into a copper mug filled with ice.
3. Top up with ginger beer.
4. Garnish with mint and a wedge of lime. Serve.

BARTENDER TIP

If you're not a huge fan of a strong ginger punch, use ginger ale instead of ginger beer. The ale has a much milder flavour.

THE LITTLE BOOK OF GIN

GINGER GIN MULE

THE LITTLE BOOK OF GIN

GIN RICKEY

GIN RICKEY

SERVES: 1 | SERVED IN: HIGHBALL GLASS

A Gin Rickey is refreshing and super easy to make. It balances a tart lime flavour with the herby and floral nature of gin. Popular in the 1920s, the Gin Rickey appears in F. Scott Fitzgerald's 1925 classic novel, *The Great Gatsby*.

YOU WILL NEED

50ml gin

25ml fresh lime juice

10ml simple syrup (optional)

100ml soda water

Wedge of lime, to garnish

METHOD

1. Fill a cocktail shaker with ice cubes and add the gin, lime juice and simple syrup.
2. Shake well until the shaker is cold to touch.
3. Strain into a chilled glass.
4. Top up with soda water and add some fresh ice cubes.
5. Garnish with a lime wedge and serve.

BARTENDER TIP

If you prefer your drinks less sweet, leave out the simple syrup. This cocktail was originally conceived as a 'zero sugar' drink.

GRAPEFRUIT, ROSEMARY AND GIN

SERVES: 1 | SERVED IN: LOWBALL GLASS

Sweet but tangy and tart, the grapefruit in this cocktail makes for a refreshing aperitif that cleanses your palette. Gin and rosemary are a perfect match, and one of the organic compounds found in juniper berries imparts a rosemary flavour. A wonderful summertime cocktail.

YOU WILL NEED

30ml gin

45ml grapefruit juice

15ml rosemary syrup

Grapefruit wedges and rosemary sprigs, to serve

For the rosemary syrup:

200g sugar

240ml water

2 large sprigs of rosemary

METHOD

1. To make the syrup, bring the water and sugar to the boil in a saucepan. Reduce to a simmer. Add the sprigs of rosemary and stir until the sugar has dissolved.

2. Take the pan off the heat and allow to fully cool. Strain into a jar or bottle. (It will keep for up to two weeks in the fridge.)

3. Add all the ingredients to a shaker filled with ice. Shake well until combined.

4. Top up with soda water and add some fresh ice cubes.

THE LITTLE BOOK OF GIN

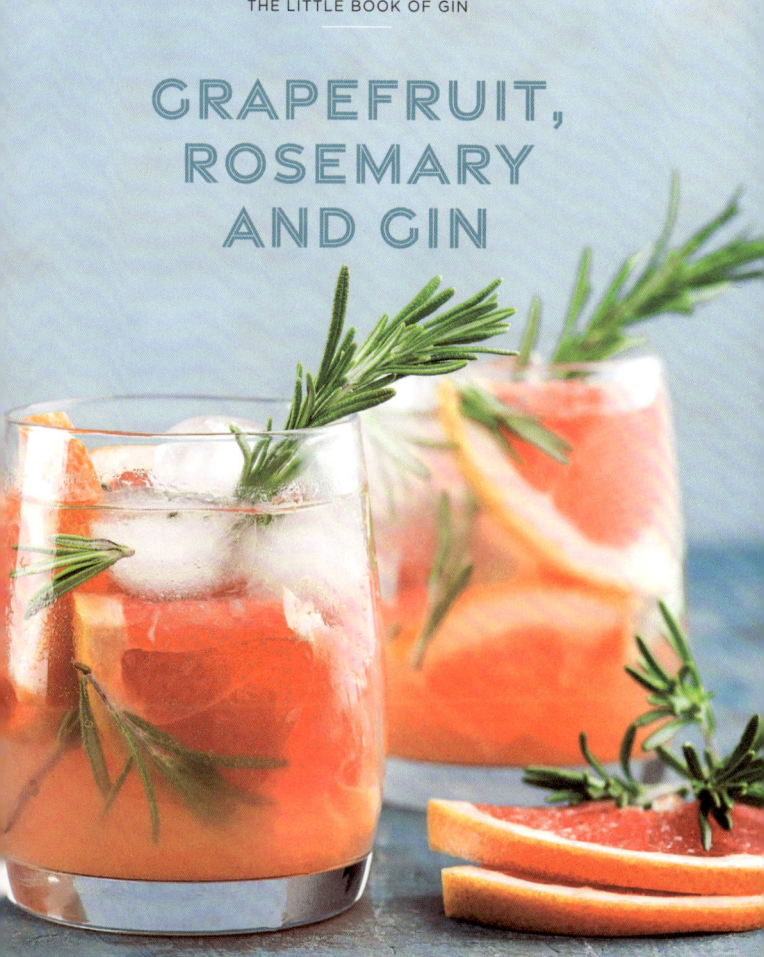

GRAPEFRUIT, ROSEMARY AND GIN

THE LITTLE BOOK OF GIN

GREYHOUND

GREYHOUND

SERVES: 1 | SERVED IN: COLLINS GLASS

This vibrant cocktail is a classic with a fruity punch. As well as looking great, it has a wonderful citrusy, tart flavour that makes it a great choice for a refreshing summer drink. Pop in a sprig of rosemary for a Mediterranean zing.

YOU WILL NEED

50ml gin

200ml freshly squeezed pink grapefruit juice

Wedge of grapefruit, slice of lime or lemon or sprig of rosemary, to garnish

METHOD

1. Put the gin and pink grapefruit juice into a cocktail shaker with a handful of ice.
2. Shake well until the outside of the shaker is cold.
3. Pour into a chilled glass with a few ice cubes.
4. Serve with a citrus garnish of your choice.

BARTENDER TIP

To create a Salty Dog, simply salt the rim of the glass. The only difference between a Greyhound and a Salty Dog is the salt.

HANKY PANKY

SERVES: 1 | SERVED IN: NICK & NORA OR COUPE GLASS

This elegant cocktail – sweet with bitter notes – was created for a customer by Ada Coleman, a bartender at London's Savoy Hotel. When the customer tried it, he said, 'By Jove! That is the real hanky panky!' and the name stuck.

YOU WILL NEED

45ml gin

45ml sweet vermouth

4.5ml Fernet-Branca (a bitter Italian digestivo)

Orange peel, to garnish

METHOD

1. In a mixing glass, add all the ingredients and then fill the glass with ice.
2. Stir and then strain into a chilled glass.
3. Garnish with a twist of orange peel.

BARTENDER TIP

A more recent version of this recipe includes a dash of orange juice. Give it a try to add a little extra zing.

THE LITTLE BOOK OF GIN

HANKY PANKY

THE LITTLE BOOK OF GIN

HONOLULU

HONOLULU

SERVES: 1 | SERVED IN: COUPE GLASS

The Honolulu was one of the signature cocktails that accompanied the golden era of 1930s Hollywood. With its tropical fruitiness, the Honolulu is a fantastic option for a hot summer's day. Basically, it's a holiday in a glass (glitz and glamour optional).

YOU WILL NEED

60ml gin

15ml pineapple juice

15ml fresh orange juice

7.5ml lemon juice

7.5ml simple syrup (see recipe on page 17)

1 dash Angostura bitters

Lemon peel

METHOD

1. Fill a cocktail shaker with ice and add all the ingredients. Shake well.
2. Strain into a chilled, sugar-rimmed glass.
3. Serve garnished with a twist of lemon peel.

BARTENDER TIP

Using the best-quality fruit juice you are able to find will ensure your cocktails taste as good as they possible can.

HOT GIN TODDY

SERVES: 1 | SERVED IN: MUG OR HEATPROOF GLASS

If you're looking for a warming winter drink, look no further than a gin toddy. The flavours of the gin are lovingly wrapped in the sweet honey and lemon notes of this cocktail. A hot toddy is often drunk as a nightcap and, according to tradition, can ease the symptoms of cold and flu.

YOU WILL NEED

45ml gin

120ml hot water

22.5ml fresh lemon juice

1 tsp honey

Cinnamon stick, to garnish

METHOD

1. Combine all the ingredients, except for the cinnamon garnish, in a mug or heatproof glass. Stir well.
2. Drop in the cinnamon stick and serve hot.

BARTENDER TIP

Experiment with the spices you add. Try cardamon, peppercorns, nutmeg or star anise to add more heat. Adding a few slices of fresh ginger will also boost the toddy's medicinal qualities!

THE LITTLE BOOK OF GIN

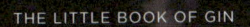

HOT GIN TODDY

THE LITTLE BOOK OF GIN

HUGO

HUGO

SERVES: 1 | SERVED IN: WINE GLASS

A fantastic aperitif, the Hugo originated in a small Alpine town in northern Italy and was inspired by the elder trees native to that area. It's an incredibly refreshing drink and very few people dislike the taste, which makes it ideal for parties or fussy friends!

YOU WILL NEED

20ml gin	120ml prosecco
20ml elderflower liqueur	6 fresh mint leaves
25ml sparkling water	2 slices of lime, to garnish

METHOD

1. Put a handful of ice cubes in a wine glass.
2. Using a pestle and mortar, gently crush the mint leaves to release the oils and flavour. Then tear the leaves and put them in the glass.
3. Add the gin, elderflower liqueur, sparkling water and lime. Stir.
4. Top up the glass with the prosecco and stir again gently. Serve.

BARTENDER TIP

For a non-alcoholic Hugo, simply replace the gin and the elderflower liqueur with elderflower syrup (or cordial) and use club soda and a dash of lemonade instead of prosecco.

JULIET AND ROMEO

SERVES: 1 | SERVED IN: COUPE OR MARTINI GLASS

Floral, herbal, refreshing and absolutely delicious, the creator of this cocktail wanted it to taste 'like a walk through an English garden' and it absolutely hits that flavour spot. The bitters, rosewater and mint leaf garnish add a final beautiful flourish.

YOU WILL NEED

½ wedge of lime (optional)

½ tbsp coarse salt, for rim of the glass (optional)

60ml gin

22.5ml lime juice

22.5ml simple syrup (see page 17)

3 slices cucumber

3 sprigs fresh mint

1 pinch salt

To garnish: 3 drops Angostura bitters, 3 drops rosewater and mint leaf

METHOD

1. OPTIONAL: Run the lime wedge around the rim of a glass and then dip the glass in the salt. Set aside.

2. In a cocktail shaker, muddle the cucumber and mint with the pinch of salt.

3. Add the remaining ingredients to the cocktail shaker. Leave for 30 seconds.

4. Add a handful of ice to the shaker. Shake vigorously until the shaker is cold. Strain into a glass.

5. Garnish with a mint leaf. Place three drops of rosewater and three drops of bitters on the surface of the drink so that they 'float'. Serve.

THE LITTLE BOOK OF GIN

JULIET AND ROMEO

THE LITTLE BOOK OF GIN

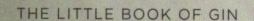

LONG ISLAND
ICED TEA

LONG ISLAND ICED TEA

SERVES: 4 | SERVED IN: COLLINS GLASS

Serve a jug of this in the garden in the summer and you'll be everyone's best friend. In theory, a Long Island Iced Tea shouldn't taste all that great given the number of different liquors involved, but there's no question it works. NOTE: there's no tea in this drink – the name comes from it being tea-coloured!

YOU WILL NEED

50ml vodka

50ml white rum

50ml tequila

50ml gin

50ml triple sec

50ml simple syrup (see recipe on page 17)

50ml fresh lemon juice

500ml cola

Lemon wedges, to garnish

METHOD

1. Add all ingredients – except the cola – to a jug. Half fill the jug with ice and stir until the outside feels cold.
2. Top with the cola and stir again.
3. Fill a glass with ice and pour. Garnish with a lemon wedge and serve with a straw.

BARTENDER TIP

If you want to make this a bit less boozy, simply cut back on the spirits (in equal measures so as not to disrupt the balance) and add extra cola in their place.

MONKEY GLAND

SERVES: 1 | SERVED IN: COUPE GLASS

The Monkey Gland was created in the 1920s by Harry MacElhone, owner of Harry's New York Bar in Paris, France. It has a sweet tart flavour with a dash of sharpness from the absinthe. The name refers to the experiments of Serge Voronoff in the 1920s where tissue from monkey testicles was grafted onto men in an attempt to boost virility!

YOU WILL NEED

60ml gin

30ml orange juice

7.5ml grenadine

Dash of absinthe

Orange slice, to garnish

METHOD

1. Swirl a dash of absinthe in a chilled glass to coat it thoroughly, then pour away the excess.
2. Add the remaining ingredients to a cocktail shaker with ice cubes. Shake well.
3. Strain into the glass and garnish with an orange slice.

BARTENDER TIP

If you prefer your cocktails less sweet, reduce the amount of grenadine or swap it for another sweetener such as honey or agave syrup.

THE LITTLE BOOK OF GIN

MONKEY GLAND

THE LITTLE BOOK OF GIN

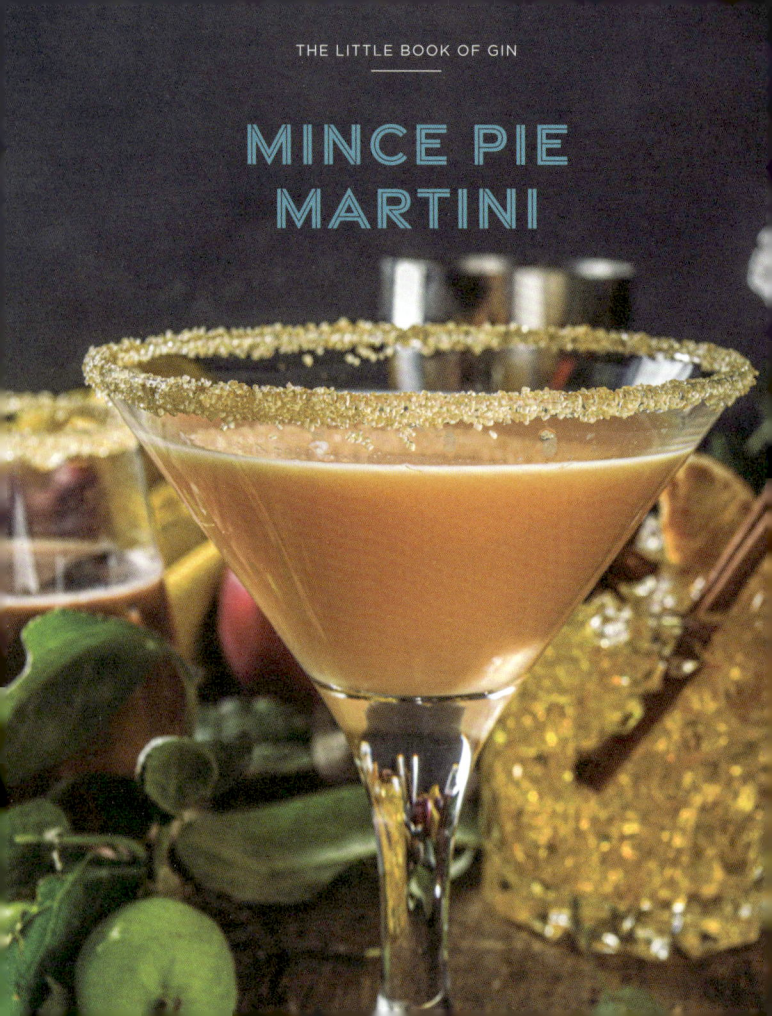

MINCE PIE MARTINI

MINCE PIE MARTINI

SERVES: 1 | SERVED IN: MARTINI GLASS

The taste of Christmas in a martini glass. You've probably never considered putting mincemeat in a cocktail before, but when you try this, you'll wonder why it's taken you so long! This delicious festive concoction will have walking in a winter wonderland in no time at all.

YOU WILL NEED

50ml gin	2 tsp mincemeat	*For the mince pie syrup*
50ml red vermouth	2 tbsp sugar	50g golden sugar
10ml dark rum	2 tsp mixed spice	25g mincemeat
		100ml water

METHOD

1. To make the mince pie syrup, heat the golden sugar, 25g of mincemeat and water in a saucepan. Simmer for five minutes, stirring until the mincemeat and sugar have dissolved. Leave to cool then strain into an airtight container. (This will keep in the fridge for a month.)

2. Combine the mixed spice and sugar on a plate. Lightly wet the rim of the glass and press into the mix to create a sugar rim.

3. Fill a cocktail shaker with ice. Add the 2 tsp of mincemeat, gin, vermouth, rum and 40ml of the mincemeat syrup, muddle and then shake well for 15 seconds.

4. Strain into a glass and serve immediately.

BARTENDER TIP

Once you've made your mince pie syrup, experiment with adding a splash to any of your favourite cocktails.

MULLED GIN

SERVES: 1 | SERVED IN: HEATPROOF GLASS OR MUG

If you think gin is just for the summer, think again. This mulled gin recipe is a great winter warmer and perfect for Christmas celebrations. You can experiment with the flavours using the recipe below as a base - try adding star anise or cloves to create your own festive treat.

YOU WILL NEED

150ml cloudy apple juice

1 cinnamon stick

Orange and lemon peel

½ tsp grated ginger

50ml gin

METHOD

1. In a small saucepan, warm the apple juice along with the cinnamon stick, orange and lemon peel and ginger.
2. When heated through, strain into a mug.
3. Add the gin and stir. Serve warm.

BARTENDER TIP

- If you're making a bigger batch for a party, scale up the ingredients and keep the apple juice, cinnamon, orange, lemon and ginger warming gently on the hob. Only add the gin when you decant the liquid into individual glasses.

THE LITTLE BOOK OF GIN

MULLED GIN

THE LITTLE BOOK OF GIN

NEGRONI

NEGRONI

SERVES: 1 | SERVED IN: LOWBALL GLASS

This is a deliciously bitter, sweet and strong cocktail that makes a perfect aperitif. The Negroni dates from around 1919, when Count Camillo Negroni asked for his usual favourite tipple to be made stronger by adding gin in place of soda water. Once a slice of orange was added, the Negroni was born.

YOU WILL NEED

30ml gin

30ml Campari

30ml sweet vermouth

1 wedge of orange

METHOD

1. Fill a cocktail shaker with ice and add the gin, Campari and vermouth.
2. Shake to mix completely. Strain into the glass.
3. Add ice and an orange wedge.

BARTENDER TIP

There are lots of Negroni variations. Make an Americano using club soda instead of gin. A Negroni Sbagliato ('mistake') swaps the gin for prosecco.

PINK NEGRONI

SERVES: 1 | SERVED IN: OLD FASHIONED GLASS

There are several recipes for making a pink negroni and this is one of the simpler versions. The recipe uses 'pink gin', which generally refers to gins that are flavoured and infused with red fruits (such as strawberries or rhubarb) during or after the distillation process.

YOU WILL NEED

30ml pink gin

30ml sweet white vermouth

15ml Aperol

Orange wheel or slice, to garnish

METHOD

1. Add the gin, vermouth and Aperol to a cocktail shaker with a handful of ice. Stir until the outside of the shaker feels cold.

2. Pour over a handful of ice in a glass.

3. Garnish with an orange wheel or slice.

BARTENDER TIP

If you prefer your cocktails to be slightly bitter, replace the Aperol with Campari.

THE LITTLE BOOK OF GIN

PINK NEGRONI

THE LITTLE BOOK OF GIN

RAMOS GIN FIZZ

RAMOS GIN FIZZ

SERVES: 1 | SERVED IN: HIGHBALL GLASS

If your inner child is a fan of milkshakes, this is the cocktail for you. The Ramos Gin Fizz is like an alcoholic milkshake, flavoured with the sweet floral tones of orange flower water.

YOU WILL NEED

- 50ml gin
- 15ml fresh lemon juice
- 15ml fresh lime juice
- 30ml simple syrup (see page 17)
- Dash of orange flower water
- 1 egg white
- 60ml cream
- Soda water

METHOD

1. Add all the ingredients (apart from the soda water) to a cocktail shaker. Dry shake (without ice) for at least two minutes to froth up the egg white.
2. Add a handful of ice to the cocktail shaker. Shake until the shaker is ice cold to touch.
3. Strain into a highball glass, over ice.
4. Top up the glass with the soda water.

BARTENDER TIP

The Ramos Gin Fizz can be quite a workout. To get the texture right, you have to shake it – a lot. Its creator, Henry Charles Ramos, would hire a shaking assistant to do this for him!

RED SNAPPER

SERVES: 1 | SERVED IN: COLLINS GLASS

A Red Snapper is basically a Bloody Mary made with gin rather than vodka and is just as good for a morning-after-the-night-before tipple. Some say the bold flavour of gin makes it even better, and it's as snappy as the name suggests.

YOU WILL NEED

50ml gin

100ml tomato juice

15ml fresh lemon juice

5ml Worcester sauce

2 pinches of salt

Slices of cucumber of a pickled gherkin, to garnish

METHOD

1. Put a handful of ice in a cocktail shaker. Add all the ingredients, apart from the garnish.
2. Stir well to mix.
3. Pour into a glass filled with ice.
4. Serve garnished with the cucumber or gherkin.

BARTENDER TIP

The more traditional garnish for a Bloody Mary is a slice of lemon and a stick of celery. Celery isn't to everyone's taste, so the cucumber in the Red Snapper is a great alternative.

THE LITTLE BOOK OF GIN

RED SNAPPER

THE LITTLE BOOK OF GIN

SINGAPORE SLING

SINGAPORE SLING

SERVES: 1 | SERVED IN: HIGHBALL GLASS

Born in Singapore in 1915, the Singapore Sling is a classic at hotels and airports. The recipe has changed a lot since its conception but this version combines gin, brandy, triple sec and Bénédictine with fruit juices and bitters for a cocktail bursting with flavour!

YOU WILL NEED

- 30ml dry gin
- 15ml cherry brandy
- 15ml lime juice
- 50ml pineapple juice
- 10ml Bénédictine
- 10ml triple sec
- Dash Angostura bitters
- Dash grenadine
- Sparkling water
- Wedge of pineapple and a Maraschino cherry, to garnish

METHOD

1. Put a handful of ice into a cocktail shaker then add all the liquid ingredients. Shake until chilled.
3. Strain into a glass over some more ice.
4. Top up with sparkling water if necessary.
5. Garnish with a wedge of pineapple and a maraschino cherry.

BARTENDER TIP

Try halving the amount of cherry brandy and replacing it with cherry liqueur for an extra sweet cherry kick.

SLIPPERY WHEN WET

SERVES: 1 | SERVED IN: ROCKS GLASS

Leave out the gin and you'd be forgiven for thinking this is a healthy smoothie. Thanks to the strawberries, it might even count as one of your five-a-day. But let's be honest, it probably doesn't so you might as well add the gin and thoroughly enjoy the naughtiness.

YOU WILL NEED

60ml gin

22.5ml fresh lemon juice

15ml honey

1 large ripe strawberry, halved

1 heaped tsp plain Greek yoghurt

Ground black pepper and a half strawberry, to garnish

METHOD

1. Put the strawberry halves, lemon juice and honey in a cocktail shaker and muddle until well broken up.
2. Add the gin and yoghurt and then fill the cocktail shaker with ice.
3. Shake for 15-20 seconds or until the shaker is cold to touch.
4. Double strain into a glass with crushed ice.
5. Garnish with the black pepper and strawberry half.

BARTENDER TIP

No fresh strawberries to hand or prefer to only use them when they're in season? Simply replace them with 2 teaspoons of strawberry jam.

THE LITTLE BOOK OF GIN

SLIPPERY WHEN WET

THE LITTLE BOOK OF GIN

SLOE GIN

SLOE GIN

MAKES: 1.5 LITRES | SERVED IN: SHERRY GLASS

Sloe gin is a liqueur made by infusing sloe berries, from the blackthorn tree, in gin. Sloes have long been enjoyed in England and make a natural pairing with gin. The longer you leave this liqueur to mature, the more richly rounded and fruity its flavour will become. If possible, make it one year ahead of when you want to drink it.

YOU WILL NEED

500g ripe sloes

250g golden caster sugar

1 litre gin

METHOD

1. Rinse the sloes and pat dry. Using a fork or cocktail stick, prick the sloes, then transfer to a 2-litre glass jar (with airtight lid).

2. Add the caster sugar and gin and then seal the jar. Shake well. For the next seven days, shake the jar well daily. Then store in a cool, dark place and leave for at least two to three months.

3. Line a sieve with a square of muslin and strain the sloe gin through it into a bowl. Decant into a bottle (or several individual bottles), seal and label.

BARTENDER TIP

Make a Sloe Royale by pouring 15ml of sloe gin into a champagne flute and topping up the glass with chilled sparkling wine or champagne. Garnish with a twist of orange peel.

SOUTHSIDE

SERVES: 1 | SERVED IN: COUPE GLASS

If you like gin and you love mojitos then this super-simple and super-refreshing cocktail is a dream come true. It will transport you to a tropical paradise with its sweet and minty flavours. Want a Southside Fizz? Simply add soda or sparkling water.

YOU WILL NEED

5 mint leaves

30ml fresh lime juice

60ml gin

30ml simple syrup

Sprig of mint, to garnish

METHOD

1. Put the mint leaves and lime juice in a cocktail shaker. Muddle gently.
2. Add the gin, simple syrup and a handful of ice. Shake until the shaker is cold to touch.
3. Double strain the mixture into a chilled glass.
4. Garnish with a sprig of mint and serve.

BARTENDER TIP

If you haven't got a fresh lime to hand, you can swap in a lemon. You'll get a slightly different taste but it will be just as delicious.

THE LITTLE BOOK OF GIN

SOUTHSIDE

THE LITTLE BOOK OF GIN

SUBLIME MOMENT

SUBLIME MOMENT

SERVES: 1 | SERVED IN: COUPE GLASS

Sweet and intense, this cocktail is for anyone who loves chocolate ... despite there being no chocolate in it! When the ingredients are mixed, something magical happens and the flavour of chocolate emerges. Don't believe us? Give it a try.

YOU WILL NEED

50ml gin

25ml fresh pink grapefruit juice

15ml vanilla simple syrup

Sprig of rosemary, to garnish

METHOD

1. Fill a cocktail shaker with ice and pour in the gin, pink grapefruit juice and syrup.
2. Shake for 30 seconds or until the shaker is cold to touch.
3. Strain into a chilled glass, add a sprig of rosemary to garnish and serve.

BARTENDER TIP

To make vanilla simple syrup, follow the recipe for simple syrup on page 17. When you remove it from the heat, scrape in the seeds from a vanilla pod, stir and leave to cool. Strain before using.

SUGAR & SPICE & EVERYTHING THING NICE

SERVES: 1 | SERVED IN: BALLOON GLASS

A long name for a long and delightfully refreshing cocktail. You'll find the 'sugar and spice' in the sugared rim of the glass. The 'everything nice' is the gin, of course. But you knew that already – it's why you bought this book!

YOU WILL NEED

- 25ml gin
- 15ml orgeat syrup (made with almonds, not suitable if you have a nut allergy)
- 85ml cranberry juice
- Orange or lemon wedges
- Cinnamon sugar

METHOD

1. Wipe the edge of the glass with a lemon wedge, then roll the rim in the cinnamon sugar to coat.
2. Squeeze the juice of the lemon wedge into a cocktail shaker then add the wedge. Pour in the gin, syrup and cranberry juice and add a handful of ice.
3. Shake well until the shaker feels cold to the touch.
4. Pour into the glass and garnish with a fresh orange or lemon wedge. Serve.

BARTENDER TIP

Want to make your own cinnamon sugar? Simply combine 100g of granulated sugar with a tablespoon of ground cinnamon. It will keep indefinitely but store it in an airtight container so it doesn't lose its potency.

THE LITTLE BOOK OF GIN

SUGAR & SPICE & EVERYTHING THING NICE

THE LITTLE BOOK OF GIN

THE GARDENER'S DAUGHTER

THE GARDENER'S DAUGHTER

SERVES: 1 | SERVED IN: COUPE GLASS

This is a lovely floral gin cocktail, thanks to the rosewater and Pavan liqueur, which is made with muscat grapes to give it a floral/fruity flavour followed by a clean, lemony aftertaste. The rhubarb syrup is a delicious addition too.

YOU WILL NEED

- 45ml gin
- 45ml Pavan liqueur
- 30ml rhubarb syrup
- 1 egg white
- 30ml fresh lemon juice
- 3 drops rosewater
- 2 dashes plum bitters
- Dried rosebuds, to garnish

METHOD

1. Add all the ingredients (except for the garnish) to a cocktail shaker. Shake vigorously for around two minutes so that the egg white creates a froth.
2. Add a handful of ice to the cocktail shaker. Shake again until the shaker is cold to touch.
3. Strain into a glass.
4. Garnish with dried rose buds and serve.

BARTENDER TIP

The exact measurement of a 'dash' or 'splash' is not important and won't make or break your drink. If you want to be precise, a dash is 0.9ml (see page 16).

THE LAST WORD

SERVES: 1 | SERVED IN: COUPE OR MARTINI GLASS

With its perfect balance of sweetness and acidity, bartenders have been making this cocktail since the pre-Prohibition era. The Last Word gets its unmistakeable green tinge from the chartreuse. Sip slowly – this is a strong one.

YOU WILL NEED

22.5ml gin

22.5ml freshly squeezed lime juice

22.5ml maraschino liqueur

22.5ml green Chartreuse

Lime wedge and cherry, to garnish

METHOD

1. Fill a cocktail shaker with ice and add all the ingredients. Shake vigorously for 15 seconds.
2. Strain into a chilled glass.
3. Serve garnished with a wedge of lime and a cherry on a skewer.

BARTENDER TIP

If you're getting bits in your drink – double strain it. Pour it through a fine-mesh strainer after straining it through the cocktail shaker's strainer.

THE LAST WORD

THE LITTLE BOOK OF GIN

TOM COLLINS

TOM COLLINS

SERVES: 1 | SERVED IN: COLLINS OR HIGHBALL GLASS

The first record of a recipe for this refreshing classic cocktail appeared in 1876. It was named after a prank that was popular in 1874 in the US. One person would say to another: 'Have you seen Tom Collins? You'd better find him as he's saying bad things about you!' The other person would then storm off in search of the non-existent Collins.

YOU WILL NEED

60ml gin

15ml simple syrup (see recipe on page 17)

15ml lemon juice

Soda water

1 lemon slice

METHOD

1. Fill the glass with ice.
2. Add all the ingredients to the glass and top up with soda water. Stir.
3. Serve garnished with a slice of lemon.

BARTENDER TIP

Try swapping the gin for another spirit to create a cocktail that is as equally delicious and elegant.

TROPICAL STRANGER

SERVES: 1 | SERVED IN: HIGHBALL GLASS

If you're a fan of tropical cocktails, this drink is one to add to your list of favourites. The refreshing limoncello, coupled with fruity pineapple and pomegranate, will transport you to a place where you can feel the sand between your toes and the sunshine on your skin.

YOU WILL NEED

40ml gin

15ml Limoncello

80ml pomegranate juice

15ml pineapple syrup

Sprig of lemon thyme, to garnish

METHOD

1. Place all the ingredients (apart from the garnish) in a cocktail shaker. Top up the shaker with ice cubes. Shake vigorously for 15 seconds.
2. Pour into a chilled glass and top with crushed ice.
3. Garnish with a sprig of lemon thyme and serve.

BARTENDER TIP

Throwing a summer party? Whip up a big batch of watermelon gin fizz – simply fill a bowl with gin and add watermelon juice until you can taste the watermelon. Add some lemon and ginger ale, mix well and decant into bottles.

THE LITTLE BOOK OF GIN

TROPICAL STRANGER

THE LITTLE BOOK OF GIN

VESPER MARTINI

VESPER MARTINI

SERVES: 1 | SERVED IN: MARTINI GLASS

This classic cocktail wasn't invented by a bartender, but by author Ian Fleming in his 1953 James Bond novel *Casino Royale*. Compared to the classic gin martini, the Vesper has a slightly sweet, bitter taste thanks to the vermouth. The vodka is a great counterbalance to the gin.

YOU WILL NEED

45ml gin

15ml vodka

10ml dry white vermouth

Lemon peel, to garnish

METHOD

1. Put all the ingredients (except the garnish) in a cocktail shaker. Fill with ice cubes. Shake for 10-15 seconds.
2. Double strain into a glass.
3. Drop in a piece of lemon peel to garnish.

BARTENDER TIP

Or perhaps this should be 'Bartender Warning'! The alcohol content of this martini is equivalent to double of just about any other cocktail. Go easy and drink responsibly.

WHITE LADY

SERVES: 1 | SERVED IN: MARTINI OR COUPE GLASS

The White Lady is a famous cocktail, credited to The Savoy's legendary bartender, Harry Craddock, in the early 1900s. Apparently, it was named after a woman Craddock knew who always wore white. It's an elegant cocktail that blends the dryness of gin with tart citrus and silky egg whites.

YOU WILL NEED

40ml gin

20ml Triple Sec

20ml lemon juice

1 egg white (optional)

Lemon peel

METHOD

1. Fill a cocktail shaker with ice. (If you're using the egg white, don't add ice to the shaker until you've mixed all the ingredients without ice.)
2. Pour in all the ingredients. Shake well.
3. Strain into the glass and garnish with a twist of lemon peel.

BARTENDER TIP

If you don't want to use egg white, you can replace it with aquafaba, a natural, plant-based egg replacement.

THE LITTLE BOOK OF GIN

WHITE LADY

THE LITTLE BOOK OF GIN

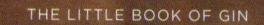

WHITE RABBIT

WHITE RABBIT

SERVES: 1 | SERVED IN: COUPE GLASS

This is a delightfully smooth amaretto cocktail. With the lemon curd, cream and vanilla, you'd be forgiven for thinking it's a liquid dessert. The White Rabbit is a firm favourite as an Easter drink but feel free to enjoy it at any time of the year.

YOU WILL NEED

- 40ml gin
- 25ml amaretto (made with almonds, not suitable if you have a nut allergy)
- 25ml double cream
- ½ tsp lemon curd
- ¼ tsp vanilla paste
- Edible flowers

METHOD

1. Put a handful of ice in a cocktail shaker and then add the gin, amaretto, double cream, lemon curd and vanilla paste. Shake until the outside of the shaker feels cold.
2. Strain the mixture into a glass.
3. Garnish with edible flowers and serve.

BARTENDER TIP

Edible flowers are a stunning garnish for cocktails and while you may be able to find them easily yourself (e.g., borage, aster, evening primrose, violas), always double check that what you pick is actually edible or buy them ready to use.

COOKING WITH GIN

COOKING WITH GIN

STARTERS
Beetroot and Gin Cured Salmon

Gin and Ginger Prawns

MAINS
Gin Marmalade Glazed Gammon

Slow Roasted Lamb with Sloe Gin

DESSERTS
Gin and Tonic Cheesecake

Strawberry and Lemon Gin Granita

BAKING
Gin and Tonic Cake

Gin Butter Cookies

THE LITTLE BOOK OF GIN

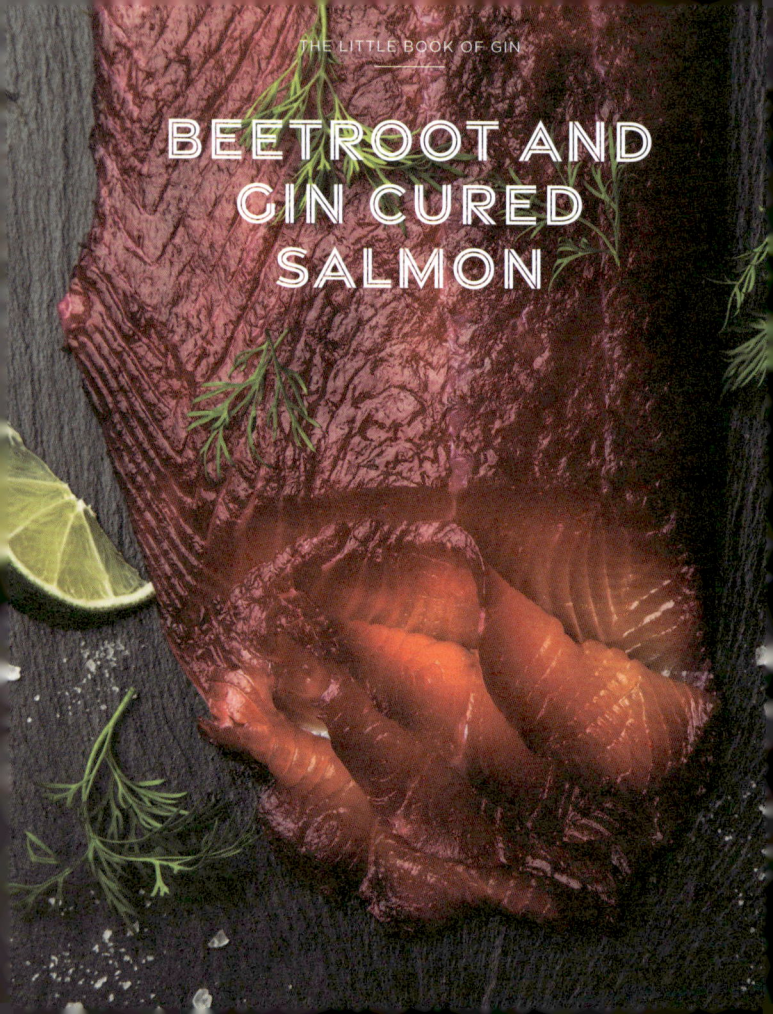

BEETROOT AND GIN CURED SALMON

BEETROOT AND GIN CURED SALMON

SERVES: 4-5 AS A STARTER
PREP PLUS CURING TIME: TWO DAYS

Beetroot and Gin Cured Salmon is a classic and elegant starter. It's easy to make and is sure to impress, both with its looks and taste. The herbs, juniper berries and gin add a delicate flavour, while the beetroot provides a great colour to this dish.

YOU WILL NEED

- 250g salmon fillet or loin
- Two large beetroots (uncooked and grated)
- Sprig of tarragon
- Sprig of thyme
- 1 tsp juniper berries, slightly crushed
- Zest of 1 lemon
- 2 tbsp rock salt
- 2 tbsp unrefined caster sugar
- 50ml gin

METHOD

1. To make the cure, combine the grated beetroot, lemon zest, salt, sugar, tarragon, thyme, juniper berries and gin.

2. Place the cure in a large stainless steel or glass container. Add the salmon and toss. Seal the container with a lid or clingfilm.

3. Put the container in a fridge for 36 to 48 hours, turning the salmon occasionally.

4. Rinse the cure from the salmon and pat the salmon dry.

5. To serve, cut the salmon into thin slices and serve with salad, bread and crème fraiche.

6. Once cured, you can keep the salmon in an airtight container in the fridge for a couple of days. It can also be frozen to use at a later date.

GIN AND GINGER PRAWNS

SERVES: 4 AS A STARTER
PREP PLUS COOKING TIME: 10 MINS

This starter is so delicious and quick to prepare, you'll make it over and over again. Cooked with butter and spring onions, and flavoured with pickled ginger, the prawns are succulent and sweet.

YOU WILL NEED

24 large prawns, peeled

60g butter

Bunch of spring onions, chopped

90g pickled ginger with pickling liquid, chopped

60ml gin

METHOD

1. Melt the butter in a frying pan over a low heat.
2. Add the spring onions and stir until slightly softened.
3. Add the prawns. Cook for 2-3 minutes or until just translucent.
4. Add the pickled ginger, 2 tbsp of pickling juice and the gin. Cook for one more minute.
5. Serve immediately in bowls, accompanied by crusty bread to mop up the juices.

COOK TIP

You can make this starter into a main course by serving it over noodles or pasta. Garnish with a handful of chopped parsley.

THE LITTLE BOOK OF GIN

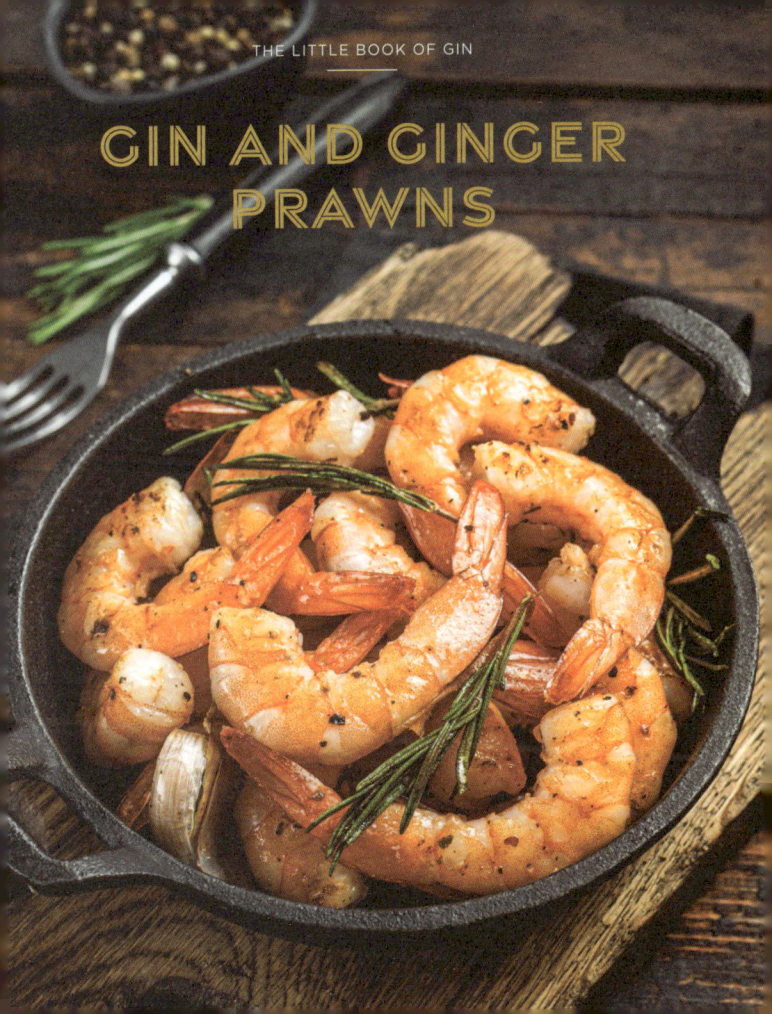

GIN AND GINGER PRAWNS

THE LITTLE BOOK OF GIN

GIN MARMALADE GLAZED GAMMON

GIN MARMALADE GLAZED GAMMON

SERVES: 6 AS A MAIN COURSE
PREP PLUS COOKING TIME: 3.5 HOURS

YOU WILL NEED

- 1.5kg gammon joint
- 1 large onion, roughly chopped
- 1 celery stick, roughly chopped
- 1 carrot, roughly chopped
- 2 bay leaves
- Cloves
- 2 tbsp orange marmalade (no peel)
- 1 tbsp dark muscovado sugar
- 1½ tbsp Dijon mustard
- 50ml gin

METHOD

1. Place the gammon in a large saucepan, cover with cold water and bring to the boil. Once boiling, add the onion, celery, carrots and bay leaves. Reduce the heat and simmer gently for 2.5 hours. Remove the gammon (now ham!) and set aside.

2. Preheat the oven to 200°C/180°C fan/gas mark 6.

3. Put the marmalade, sugar and mustard in a small saucepan over a gentle heat. Stir until everything has melted. Remove from the heat and stir in the gin.

4. Remove the skin on the ham and score the fat with a knife to make diamond shapes. Stud each diamond with a clove.

5. Spread the glaze over the ham and roast in the oven for 45 minutes, occasionally adding more glaze. Serve with green vegetables and potatoes.

6. This is also delicious served cold in sandwiches or with chutney and pickles.

SLOW ROASTED LAMB WITH SLOE GIN

SERVES: 4 | PREP PLUS COOKING TIME: 3.5 HOURS

The sweet and fruity taste of sloe gin with its berry flavours and slight tartness is a wonderful addition to the richness of lamb. This is a simple way to up your Sunday roast game, as well as enjoy your favourite tipple.

YOU WILL NEED

1.3kg leg and shoulder of lamb	2 large red onions, peeled and quartered	150ml sloe gin
2 tbsp fresh mint, chopped	1 tbsp olive oil	Salt and pepper, to season

METHOD

1. Preheat the oven to 160°C/140°C fan/gas mark 3.
2. Score the skin of the lamb with a sharp knife and rub in the mint, plus seasoning.
3. Place the onions in a large roasting tin. Sit the joint on top of the onions, drizzle with the oil and sloe gin.
4. Cover with foil and roast in the oven for 2.5-3 hours, basting occasionally with the juices. Remove the foil for the last 30 minutes of roasting.
5. Remove from the oven and leave to rest for 10 minutes.
6. Serve with roast potatoes and vegetables.

COOK TIP

Removing the foil from the meat towards the end of the cooking period will allow the meat to brown.

THE LITTLE BOOK OF GIN

SLOW ROASTED LAMB WITH SLOE GIN

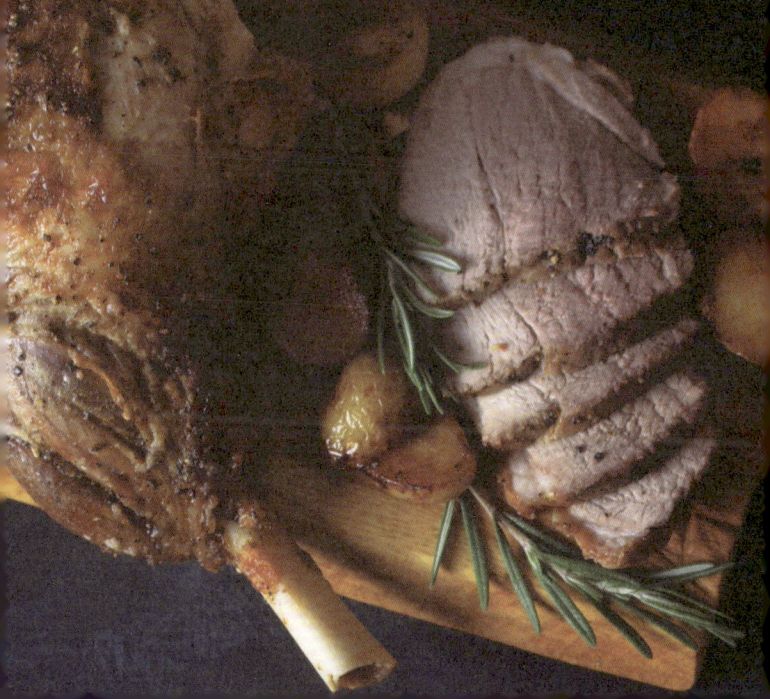

THE LITTLE BOOK OF GIN

GIN AND TONIC
CHEESECAKE

GIN AND TONIC CHEESECAKE

SERVES: 8
PREP PLUS COOKING TIME: 35 MINS + 5-6 HOURS TO SET

This refreshing cheesecake is no-bake and is super easy to make. It has a delicious buttery biscuit base topped with a creamy gin and tonic filling.

YOU WILL NEED

- 300g digestive biscuits
- 150g unsalted butter
- 125ml gin
- 125ml tonic water
- 75g caster sugar
- 5 gelatine leaves
- 600g full fat cream cheese
- 450ml double cream
- 100g icing sugar
- Juice of half a lime
- Lime zest

METHOD

1. Put the biscuits in a food processor and blend into fine crumbs. Melt the butter and then mix into the biscuits. Transfer the biscuit mix to a lined 8"/20cm tin and press down firmly. Refrigerate.

2. Soak the gelatine leaves in cold water for five minutes. Remove and set aside. Put the gin, tonic water and caster sugar in a saucepan and heat until the sugar dissolves. Add the gelatine and stir until dissolved. Remove from the heat.

3. Whisk together the cream cheese, icing sugar and lime juice until smooth. Slowly mix in the gin mixture. Add 300ml of double cream and whisk again. Spoon over the biscuit mixture. Leave to set in the fridge for 5-6 hours.

4. Whisk together the remaining double cream and icing sugar until smooth. Spoon onto the cheesecake and sprinkle with lime zest. Serve.

STRAWBERRY AND LEMON GIN GRANITA

SERVES: 4 | PREP PLUS COOKING TIME: 10 MINS + 4 HOURS FOR FREEZING

Granita is a frozen dessert from Sicily, made with water, sugar and various flavours. The texture is similar to sorbet, but with a slightly grainy crunch thanks to its ice crystals. It's a refreshing way to end a meal and with the addition of gin, this dessert will certainly ignite your tastebuds.

YOU WILL NEED

| 400g fresh strawberries, stalks removed and halved | 60ml simple syrup (see page 17) | 60ml gin
Zest and juice of half a lemon |

METHOD

1. Put the strawberries, simple syrup, gin, zest and lemon juice in a blender. Blend for 45 to 60 seconds.
2. Pour the mixture into a metal roasting tray (with sides) and put in the freezer for around 30 minutes, or until ice starts to form around the edges.
3. Mix with a fork and then freeze for a further 30 minutes. Repeat this process every 30 minutes over 4-6 hours until the granita is icy.
4. Serve immediately in pretty glasses.

COOK TIP

You don't need to stick to strawberries when making this recipe. Other fruits, such as raspberries, blackberries or peaches, are equally delicious individually or as a combination.

THE LITTLE BOOK OF GIN

STRAWBERRY AND LEMON GIN GRANITA

THE LITTLE BOOK OF GIN

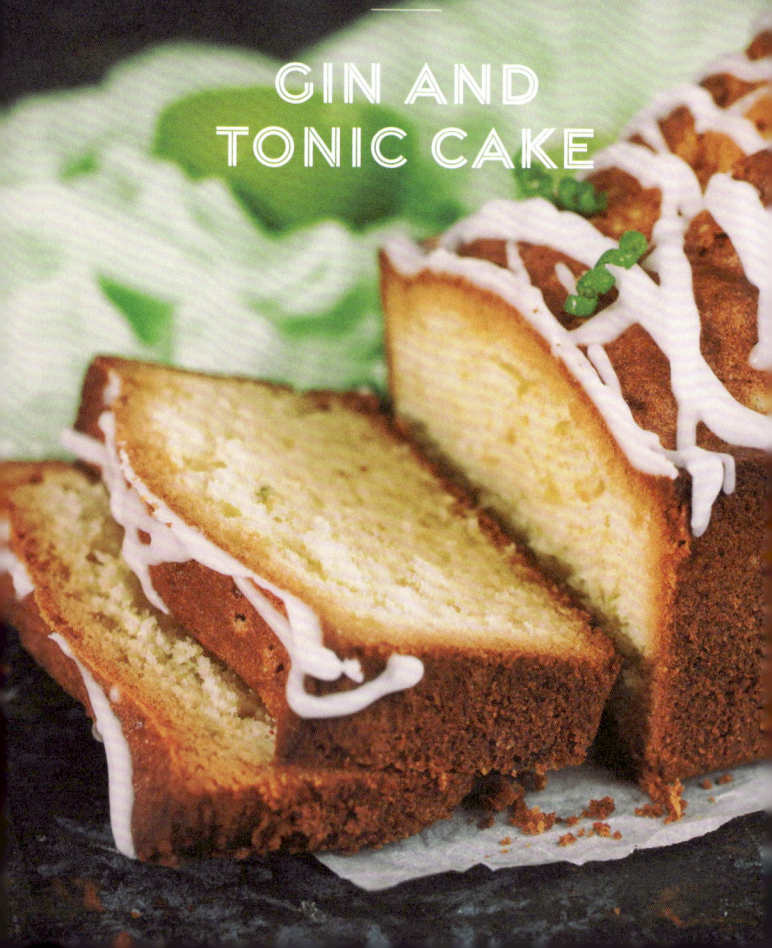

GIN AND TONIC CAKE

GIN AND TONIC CAKE

SERVES: 12 | PREP PLUS COOKING TIME: 1 HOUR

Who knew it? A gin and tonic cake?! This cake is totally delicious and is a guaranteed people pleaser. Just go easy with the measures - it is pretty boozy, especially if you opt to finish it off with gin icing too.

YOU WILL NEED

- 360g plain flour
- 2 tsp baking powder
- ¼ tsp salt
- 225g unsalted butter
- 350g caster sugar
- 4 large eggs
- 2 tsp vanilla extract
- 1½ tbsp lime zest
- 135ml gin
- 60ml milk
- 110g icing sugar
- Juice of two limes

METHOD

1. Preheat oven to 180°C/160°C fan/gas mark 4.
2. In a large bowl, mix together the flour, baking powder and salt.
3. In a separate bowl, beat together the butter and caster sugar until creamy. Slowly beat in the eggs. Mix in the vanilla and lime zest.
4. Combine the two bowls of ingredients and mix well. Stir in 60ml of the gin, milk and half the lime juice. Transfer to a greased baking dish and bake for 35-40 minutes, until the top is golden.
5. To make the glaze, combine the remaining gin and lime juice and add the icing sugar. Using a fork, make holes in the top of the cake and pour the glaze over. Leave to cool completely before serving.

COOK TIP

Add even more gin to this cake by finishing it off with gin icing. Combine 2-3 tbsp gin with 155g icing sugar and and spread smoothly.

GIN BUTTER COOKIES

SERVES: MAKES AROUND 24 COOKIES
PREP PLUS COOKING TIME: 20 MINUTES

Fear not, the alcohol burns off when these cookies are baked, leaving behind the lovely herby botanical flavours of gin. Why not bake a batch as a homemade gift for the gin lover in your life?

YOU WILL NEED

115g unsalted butter	180g plain flour	Pinch of salt
100g caster sugar	30ml gin	Brown sugar for dusting
1 egg	½ tsp baking powder	

METHOD

1. Preheat oven to 180°C/160°C fan/gas mark 4.
2. Blend the butter and sugar together until creamy. Add the egg and mix until light and fluffy.
3. Add the flour, gin, baking powder and salt and mix until it forms a dough. Wrap the dough in clingfilm and chill in the fridge for two hours.
4. Roll out the dough to 1cm thick. Cut out the cookies and place on a lined baking sheet. Dust with sugar.
5. Bake for 8-10 minutes. Remove from oven and transfer to a wire rack to cool completely.

COOK TIP

Try making these with lavender for an extra floral pop. Simply stir in 1tbsp of dried lavender buds at the same time as adding the flour.

THE LITTLE BOOK OF GIN

GIN BUTTER COOKIES

OTHER USES FOR GIN

OTHER USES FOR GIN

Gin may be a delicious drink, but did you know that it has a versatile range of non-edible and non-drinkable uses? Here are some more reasons why gin is so useful to have around the home!

MULTIPURPOSE CLEANER

Gin is fantastic for cleaning around the house. (Although don't use an expensive brand!). Simply put some in a spray bottle and off you go. It's especially good for cleaning mirrors and glass when missed with water, and if you've got any spots of mould or mildew, it can remove that too. Just spray it on and leave for five minutes, before wiping away with a damp cloth.

CLEANING JEWELLERY

This works best on plain metal or diamond-set jewellery – avoid using gin on gemstones or pearls. Just submerge your jewellery in a small glass of gin and leave for 20 minutes. Give the liquid a swirl every five minutes. The gin will clean dirt from the nooks and crannies and restore your jewellery's sparkle.

ANTI-FUNGAL FOOTBATH

Gin has natural anti-fungal properties, so is perfect for tending to less-than-perfect feet. Mix half a cup of gin into a large bowl of warm water and soak your feet for ten minutes. It's by no means a miracle cure but it may help fungal conditions, and make your feet smell more pleasant.

CARPET STAIN REMOVAL

We all know about white wine and salt for combatting red wine spills, but if you don't have these to hand, try gin. To remove a red wine stain on carpet or upholstery, pour some gin on the stain and then dab it with a clean, dry cloth. Repeat this a few times and the stain should start to fade. If it's a stubborn stain, add baking soda at the end, leave overnight, dab with white vinegar in the morning and then vacuum.

UPCYCLE YOUR GIN BOTTLE

If you love gin and get through a few bottles, don't throw them in the recycling bin – upcycle them. There are lots of great ways to re-use bottles, particularly those with beautifully designed labels. Make a lamp base, fill them with fairy lights and use them as vases. You can also fill your empty bottle with 350ml of mineral oil and 50 drops of essential oil and pop a few reed sticks in the top – hey presto, your very own room diffuser!

HANDWASH

Another way to upcycle an empty bottle is to turn it into a soap dispenser. Buy a pump or reuse one from an existing bottle that will fit, then simply add your favourite liquid soap. You can also add a few tablespoons of gin to the soap too – the juniper in the gin has natural anti-bacterial properties.

OTHER USES FOR GIN

AIR FRESHENER

Do you have one gin that you absolutely LOVE the smell of? Use it to make an air freshener so that you can enjoy the aroma every day. Simply fill a spray bottle with 30ml gin, 120ml filtered water and 20-40 drops of your favourite essential oil and spritz it around the room. Don't worry, your home won't smell like a bar – the alcohol quickly evaporates to leave behind the botanical smell you love.

SMELLY SHOES

The anti-fungal and anti-bacterial properties of gin make it a perfect treatment for stinky shoes. Not only will they smell wonderful, but you'll also blitz nasty odour-causing bacteria. Just put some gin in a spray bottle, spray the insides of the shoes and leave overnight to dry.

GIN QUOTES

GIN QUOTES

'A perfect martini should be made by filling a glass with gin then waving it in the general direction of Italy.'

Noel Coward

'My main ambition as a gardener is to water my orange trees with gin. Then all I have to do is squeeze the juice into a glass.'

W C Fields

'Fortunately, there is gin, the sole glimmer in this darkness. Do you feel the golden, copper-coloured light it kindles in you? I like walking through the city of an evening in the warmth of gin.'

Albert Camus

'The sooner the tea's out the way, the sooner we can get out the gin.'

Henry Reed

'I have seen my kid struggle into the kitchen in the morning with outfits that need only one accessory: an empty gin bottle.'

Erma Bombeck

'The gin and tonic has saved more Englishmen's lives, and minds, than all the doctors in the Empire.'

Winston Churchill

'The proper union of gin and vermouth is a great and sudden glory; it is one of the happiest marriages on earth, and one of the shortest lived.'

Bernard DeVoto

'Red meat and gin.'

Julia Child, on the secret of a long life